Provebs 25:2

Dr Ja~

A 31 DAY DEVOTIONAL

DR. JASON HIMMELBERGER

PROVERBS

A 31 DAY DEVOTIONAL

Dr. Jason Himmelberger

ISBN: 978-1-66782-862-6

Table of Contents

Chapter One

Why would I read Proverbs every day?

Their purpose is to teach, leading us to success.

Proverbs 1:2–4 (New Living Translation)

Their purpose is to teach people wisdom and discipline, to help them understand the insights of the wise. Their purpose is to teach people to live disciplined and successful lives, to help them do what is right, just, and fair. These verses will give insight to the simple, knowledge and discernment of the young.

Why? What is the point? Everyday? Really?

We all have questions. In these verses, the Bible gives us the answer right at the beginning of the book, showing its importance. These proverbs are for anyone who will listen. No matter if you are young, old, educated, or uneducated, these questions are here for you to help lead a successful life. One more abundant than you could ever come up with on your own. That is their purpose, along with the discipline to read daily and apply the basic principles, so that you might grow into the things that God has for you.

Truth: God wants you to be successful!

Declaration: God created me to be successful.

Application: Develop a daily schedule to read Proverbs

Notes:

_____

_____

_____

_____

_____

_____

_____

_____

_____

_____

_____

_____

_____

_____

_____

Chapter Two

Wisdom calls for a hearing, are you listening?

Check, check, I hear you loud and clear.

Proverbs 2:2–4 (New Living Translation)
Tune your ears to wisdom, and concentrate on understanding. Cry out for insight, and ask for understanding. Search for them as you would for silver; seek them like hidden treasures.

Tune? Concentrate? Cry? Really?

When God built us, He built us an antenna (prayer), through which we are constantly receiving information. The system that God has built as far as transmitting and receiving is so strong. We are able to pick up other signals even if they are not heavenly. Let me share a quick example. Have you ever been singing a song in your head, then got into your car, turned on the radio, and *bam*, that song was playing on the radio?

One of the reasons for reading proverbs every day and growing in wisdom, knowledge, and discernment is that we might be able to discern what signals we are transmitting and receiving. We must make sure that they are in alignment with heaven itself.

Much like an old radio that has a dial, some of us are so close to the actual radio station of heaven, but we're just a couple of numbers off. For example: In my hometown, we have a radio station that comes through good, and it is 100.3. I'm proposing that most of us are at 100.0 or 100.7.

Reading the Book of Proverbs daily helps to tune our ears to the things of heaven. This practice will help us get to the actual radio station of heaven, helping us hear the heartbeat and the instructions that God is putting forth for us on a daily basis.

Truth: God wants to reveal his heart and plans to you!

Declaration: I am locked into the frequency of heaven, and I hear the heartbeat of the father.

Application: Follow the life-giving promptings of the Holy Spirit. Step out and pray for the person across the room, in the grocery store, or even at the gas station.

Notes:

_____

_____

_____

_____

_____

_____

_____

_____

_____

_____

_____

_____

_____

_____

_____

_____

Chapter Three

Joy and wisdom

Wisdom is profitable.

Proverbs 3:13–17 (New Living Translation)

Joyful is the person who finds wisdom, the one who gains understanding. For wisdom is more profitable than silver, and her wages are better than gold. Wisdom is more precious than rubies; nothing you desire can compare with her. She offers you long-life in her right hand, and riches and honor in her left. She will guide you down delightful paths; all her ways are satisfying.

Better than gold? Long life? Cry? Guidance?

First off, this is not just a prosperity verse, it is way more than that. I want you to think of being rich in the following areas; relationships, favor, health, a particular skill (that is hard for others). So many of us are longing to be happier, even if it's in just a single area of our lives. God's wisdom can help with that. Through observation, I have found that most people tend to put the cart before the horse.

We want happiness or finances now; however, we are unwilling to take the steps to get there. We just want it. We suffer from a microwave mentality.

Wisdom, knowledge, and discernment will help get us to the Godly things we desire, ultimately bringing us joy. So even though it may seem counter intuitive, go after wisdom before you go after the gold. Wisdom will teach you how to create "gold" that will enrich your life and the lives of those around you.

DR. JASON HIMMELBERGER

Truth: Wisdom wants me to prosper!

Declaration: I am prosperous in all I do!

Application: Practice being profitable by stewarding the things you already have, i.e., your health, relationships, and finances. Are you giving ten percent to your home church? If not, start now.

Notes:

_____

_____

_____

_____

_____

_____

_____

_____

_____

_____

_____

_____

_____

_____

_____

Chapter Four

Take my words to heart and follow my commands

On your mark, get set, ready, go!

Proverbs 4:25–27 (New Living Translation)
Look straight ahead, and fix your eyes on what lies before you.
Mark out a straight path for your feet; stay on the safe path.
Don't get sidetracked; keep your feet from following evil.

Are my headlights on? Am I on track? Whom am I following? Where am I going?

Many times in my life, I have had a desire or goal. Rather than making definitive plans to achieve that goal, I will just make mental notes. Does this sound familiar? Time goes by, and I do not remember what the goal or desire was.

This is why it is so important for us to write down the goal and desires that we have to ensure that we are staying on track; that way, if anything comes against that goal, we can say "Not today, Satan" and stay on the path of righteousness, ultimately staying on track and in the fast lane.

Truth: You are called to be a prudent person! (Prudent—a person giving forethought to their future, looking ahead)

Declaration: I see the things in front of me, and I move appropriately.

Application: In the morning, give thought to your day and what the Lord has for you specifically. Make a plan. As you go about your day, look out for pitfalls that will get you off course.

Notes:

_____

_____

_____

_____

_____

_____

_____

_____

_____

_____

_____

_____

_____

_____

_____

_____

Chapter Five

Enjoy the fruit of your labor!

Stay Away!!!

Proverbs 5:7–12 (New Living Translation)

So now, my sons, listen to me. Never stray from what I am about to say: Stay away from her! Don't go near the door of her house! If you do, you will lose your honor and will lose to merciless people all you have achieved. Strangers will consume your wealth, and someone else will enjoy the fruit of your labor. In the end, you will groan in anguish when disease consumes your body. You will say, "How I hated discipline! If only I had not ignored all the warnings!

Wait for what? Do I have to wait until I'm married? Can't I have a casual relationship?

Why was this passage put in this devotional? Everyone and every generation seem to have encountered this topic in one way or another. We have a name for this type of lifestyle; you know what I'm talking about. The lifestyle when you go from girlfriend to girlfriend or a boyfriend to boyfriend, and we have all known somebody who has been affected by adultery. In the current world of theology, it is okay for you to be sleeping around; however, in regards to biblical theology and biblical standard, God calls us to live holy lifestyles, in covenant and commitment to one person.

And, yes, that means that you have to wait to have sex until you're married. Or in the case of adultery, you have to stay true to the commitment that you have made to your spouse; otherwise, you will lose everything. The context in this passage is relationally, physically, financially, and even emotionally. It's going to cost, and it's going to hurt. Don't do it.

DR. JASON HIMMELBERGER

Truth: I am designed for a life of holiness!

Declaration: I can live in contrast with the world and alignment with heaven, living a life of covenant.

Application: If not doing so already, make sure that your interactions with the opposite sex are appropriate.

Notes:

_____

_____

_____

_____

_____

_____

_____

_____

_____

_____

_____

_____

_____

_____

Chapter Six

Wake up, Wake up!

Wakey wakey it's time to get up!

Proverbs 6:6–11 (New Living Translation)
Take a lesson from the ants, you lazybones. Learn from their ways and become wise! Though they have no prince or governor or ruler to make them work, they labor hard all summer, gathering food for the winter. But you, lazybones, how long will you sleep? When will you wake up? A little extra sleep, a little more slumber, a little folding of the hands to rest—then poverty will pounce on you like a bandit; scarcity will attack you like an armed robber.

Did you just call me lazy? So I can't sleep in every day? Can't I just Netflix and chill?

To me, this is such an encouraging portion of scripture about how something so small does things that "intelligent" people do. Ants achieve such great things by working together. If an ant can do it, then surely I can do it! While I was working on my doctorate, I battled with negative self-talk. I have to remind myself that this high school dropout could "do this." The key is a physical discipline, as in getting up early every single day going to work, school, etc.

Putting in the work daily, so in hard times, I will have more than enough to make it through. I understand that this is easier said than done; however, Proverbs helped me out in so many ways.

Over time, I have developed good habits that have helped me become a better leader, student, husband, and father. You see, the word of God read

DR. JASON HIMMELBERGER

over and over does not get boring; in contrast, it gets in you, changing you little by little and day by day. Over time, you will grow in Godly wisdom, which will help you in all that you do.

Truth: I am able! God loves to give me the godly desires of my heart!

Declaration: I am not lazy; I can do the work required and more!

Application: Start by getting up one hour earlier, if possible, every single day so that you might be more productive. Do the things that you have been putting off.

Notes:

_____

_____

_____

_____

_____

_____

_____

_____

_____

_____

_____

_____

_____

Chapter Seven

Follow the leader? Wait, who is leading?

Come with me if you want to live!

Proverbs 7:1–5 (New Living Translation)

(Paraphrased in context to apply to both genders)

Follow my advice, my child; always treasure my commands. Obey my commands and live! Guard my instructions as you guard your own eyes. Tie them on your fingers as a reminder. Write them deep within your heart. Love wisdom like a sibling; make insight a beloved member of your family. Let them protect you from an affair with an immoral person, from listening to the flattery of a promiscuous person.

I'm standing guard! Wait! What are we looking for again?

Simply put, if you do follow the advice in this passage, you are going to live a much better life! Better than you can even imagine. Guarding God's instruction is like when, we protect our sight, from the sun by wearing sunglasses. Or shielding our eyes with safety glasses while doing projects like chopping wood; keeping them free of debris so we can see obstacles and navigate around them without stumbling. Treasuring the advice of the Lord is the same thing; however, it applies to everything we do. This book includes instructions that God wants us to pay attention to. He instructs to write them deep within your heart. Keep them safe. Don't forget. I like to think of our hearts as the lockbox of our lives. Don't be captivated by flattery; be careful. Using wisdom and insight you will begin to discern who does not have your best interest at heart allowing you time to protect yourself. Wisdom and insight will protect you.

DR. JASON HIMMELBERGER

Truth: It's easy to enjoy the benefits of God's advice in my life.

Declaration: I am standing guard, and yet ready and open to Godly encouragement.

Application: I will talk with a friend or leader about how to be successful and on guard with my relationships.

Notes:

_____

_____

_____

_____

_____

_____

_____

_____

_____

_____

_____

_____

_____

_____

_____

_____

Chapter Eight

Can you hear me now? Good . . .

HEY, is this thing on? Can you hear me?

Proverbs 8:1–9 (New Living Translation)

Listen as Wisdom calls out! Hear as understanding raises her voice! On the hilltop along the road, she takes her stand at the crossroads. By the gates at the entrance to the town, on the road leading in, she cries aloud, "I call to you, to all of you! I raise my voice to all people. You simple people, use good judgment. You foolish people, show some understanding. Listen to me! For I have important things to tell you. Everything I say is right, for I speak the truth and detest every kind of deception. My advice is wholesome. There is nothing devious or crooked in it. My words are plain to anyone with understanding, clear to those with knowledge."

Can you hear it, wisdom calling out to you? Are you receiving?

All through Proverbs, you will see a theme—wisdom, knowledge, and discernment. Over and over you will hear of this phraseology. Wisdom, knowledge, and discernment are prophetic pictures of the Godhead. Wisdom = Father, Knowledge = Jesus, Discernment = Holy Spirit. The Godhead is calling out to you, attempting to communicate with you for your benefit. Heaven is constantly transmitting its signal, much like Morse code.

Morse code was used in several ways. One as a basic way of communication. Even a great distances, ships are able to communicate with blasts of lights representing long or short dashes. The heavenly signal is able to be received

　　　DR. JASON HIMMELBERGER

by you, giving you insight into your day, and it's even specific to the season that you are in right now. Help is right there…Can you hear it? Slow down, listen for it.

Truth: I was made to hear God!

Declaration: God speaks to me, and I can hear Him!

Application: Throughout the day, just ask this simple question: Lord what are you saying right now? Be ready to listen, as long as it's life-giving and not life-stealing, write it down and pray on it!

<u>**Notes:**</u>

_____

_____

_____

_____

_____

_____

_____

_____

_____

_____

_____

_____

_____

Chapter Nine

Party Invitation

I'm throwing a party, and you're invited!

Proverbs 9:1–6 (New Living Translation)

Wisdom has built her house; she has carved its seven columns.

She has prepared a great banquet, mixed the wines, and set the table. She has sent her servants to invite everyone to come. She calls out from the heights overlooking the city. "Come in with me," she urges the simple. To those who lack good judgment, she says, "Come, eat my food, and drink the wine I have mixed. Leave your simple ways behind, and begin to live; learn to use good judgment."

What do you need to leave behind? What does really "living" look like for you?

Each month, as I go through proverbs, I try to assess the things that I need to let go of. The things that are weighing me down. This could be spiritually, physically, emotionally, and even relationally. It is important to keep short accounts of all that we do, making it easier to leave the simple, unnecessary ways behind. When I look at that last sentence of the verse that says "begin to live," I know that God's version of living is better than anything that I could ever come up with. As I go after more of him I learn that he is always guiding me into smother places. I say smoother because they may not be perfect with my current understanding, however, with his perspective, its good!

Truth: I am invited to the table of HIS presence!

Declaration: I will live each day as though I was invited to the party!

Application: Thank God each morning for the personal invitation to partake of HIS presence simply by recognizing the small and the big things in your life.

Notes:

_____

_____

_____

_____

_____

_____

_____

_____

_____

_____

_____

_____

_____

_____

Chapter Ten

I got a river of life flowing out of me!

Floating down the river of life

Proverbs 10:11 (New Living Translation)
The words of the Godly are a life-giving fountain; the words of
the wicked conceal violent intentions.

Am I a fountain to those around me? Are people encouraged after hanging out with me?

This is a fun one (insert sarcasm). It's really hard to do a self-assessment; some of our basic responses to various situations throughout the day when they are happening on a subconscious level. The way you handle your wrong order at the restaurant or the person tailgating you on the road.

Our Responses are really hard to manage without some deep changes. I just want to encourage you; you can do it. I would recommend asking a close friend or spouse. I did this, and I found that I was inadvertently discouraging those around me by my playful remarks.

To this day, it is something I have to keep an eye on. Although I'm just trying to be funny, it's not always a river of life that is flowing out of me.

Fountains are cool to look at, the designs that the water makes while moving from pool to pool or the arches fountains make as the water is flying through the air.

The Bellagio in Las Vegas is famous for its fountain. I have been there several times over the years; my wife just loves it. We have a pretty cool fountain in our city center, nothing like the Bellagio but cool nonetheless.

Years ago, as a high school prank, some seniors filled it with dish soap and Jell-O.

DR. JASON HIMMELBERGER

The beautiful fountain in our city that was relaxing and refreshing to all those around all of a sudden became corrupt, as soap suds and Jell-O were all along the walkway. It was so bad that you had to stay away until the city cleared it all and cleaned out the pumps. It is the same with our lives when our words are harsh and foul, tearing down those around us rather than building them up; it's like our fountain gets soap and jello in it, and it's no longer life-giving, and people have to stay away.

Truth: I was made to be a life-giving fountain with my words!

Declaration: I am an encourager to those around me!

Application: Before speaking to a friend or loved one, speak the word over yourself, if it's life-giving, then speak it. Yes, your responses will be slower. They will hit harder and make more of an impact, blessing you and your friend.

Notes:

_____

_____

_____

_____

_____

_____

_____

_____

_____

Chapter Eleven

I love my city!

The blessing of words that become reality

Proverbs 11:11 (New Living Translation)
Upright citizens are good for a city and make it prosper, but the talk of the wicked tears it apart.

The place is boring; there is nothing to do! This city is run down?

How do I speak about my city? Do I contribute to my city prospering? Upright citizens are good for a city. When you are obeying the law, paying your taxes and submitting to the authority above you (assuming they are not tyrannical leaders to keep in context), loving your city, and speaking well about the place you live prospers and benefits your city.

When you are living outside of these parameters, you are contributing to tearing your city apart. As we dive into kingdom principles, this goes into our words as well, what are you speaking in regards to your city? Our words either build our city up or tear it down, and negative talk about your city is no different. What you focus on, you will see manifest (Proverbs 4:23–27).

I used to do this myself. I had a bittersweet feeling toward life in Clallam County; yes, some things are lacking, but this area is amazing! People from all over the globe come to visit this place. The fingerprints of God are visible in every direction you look! Mountains, ocean, rainforest, etc. Speak blessings and be a blessing to your city.

Truth: We were created to bless our city!

Declaration: _____ is blessed prosperous city. I see God's presence everywhere I go.

Application: As you go about your day, drive around, pray and release a blessing over any area of your city and just watch as God moves in that area. Specifically, areas that you have recently had frustrations about. See what God does!

Notes:

_____

_____

_____

_____

_____

_____

_____

_____

_____

_____

_____

_____

_____

_____

_____

Chapter Twelve

I want to be like a tree!

Plant me by streams of living water.

Proverbs 12:3 (New Living Translation)
Wickedness never brings stability, but the godly have deep roots.

Am I wicked? How do I get stability in my life (emotionally, physically, relationally, and financially)? How do I get deep roots?

If there is no stability in areas of your life (household, relationship, finances, etc.), you may need to do a self-assessment and see if you are partnering with wickedness. Hold tight; stay with me; let me address this "wickedness" terminology real quick. God has set up this perfect place (heaven) for us to live and dwell. Only things that resemble his kingdom are there. It's like the supermarket of heaven; they only stock what heaven has.

It's perfect, righteous, and holy. Wickedness does not exist there, so anything outside of those "perfect" parameters is "wicked."

That being said, maybe you lose your temper or look at porn. When you do these things, you step outside the kingdom parameters, and that is wickedness, and it will never bring stability to your household. It causes chain reactions in other areas of your life. Just do an honest assessment to see if you are partnering with some sort of pattern of sin knowingly or unknowingly. God is graceful; just repent. You need to come to terms with it so that you can address it and move back into alignment with God's kingdom. Deep roots in Jesus keep us steady.

Truth: I was designed to live within God's parameters.

Declaration: I am a tree planted by a stream of living water; my roots are going deeper and deeper with each encounter with the Lord!

Application: Talk with a friend or leader about some areas that you need to make some adjustments in and take the appropriate steps to live free in those areas!

Notes:

_____

_____

_____

_____

_____

_____

_____

_____

_____

_____

_____

_____

_____

_____

_____

_____

_____

Chapter Thirteen

Foot to mouth syndrome

Did I just say that out loud?

Proverbs 13:3 (New Living Translation)
Those who control their tongue will have a long life; opening your mouth can ruin everything.

How do I tame this thing? I just seem to blurt this out? Oops, I did it again!

We have probably all been in a situation where we wished we would not have said anything or wanted a do-over. This was a big hurdle for me. I grew up in a rough environment where words were like weapons and shots were fired daily. As a young father, I saw that I was beginning to repeat the cycle with my children and my wife. I made the decision that my words would no longer be weapons. This behavior would have to stop with me.

Man, this process was tough to walkout. It took time, and I still have to be on guard, and there are days that I fail; however, as you control your tongue, you will see an increase in wisdom, knowledge, and discernment being active in your life. You keep your blood pressure down and tend to keep the peace a little longer. Those who are not letting their temper control them are going to have less frustrating incidents occurring in day-to-day life. Just remember this is a life-long journey.

How did I get better? Well, I read Proverbs every day. I have done this for years and years. As I feel myself getting stressed, I bite my tongue, not to the point of pain, but just as a gentle reminder to be quiet. Very much like a positivity bracelet or something of that nature. I have seen so many breakthroughs in this area of my life. If I can do it, you can too.

Truth: God has equipped me to respond rather than react!

Declaration: I speak the right things at the right times!

Application: As a gentle reminder, bite your tongue again and again, along with permitting some close friends to cut you off mid-sentence to "help" you from saying something that does not line up with your heart.

Notes:

_____

_____

_____

_____

_____

_____

_____

_____

_____

_____

_____

_____

_____

_____

_____

Chapter Fourteen

Recalculating, where in the world am I?

Man, I just want to figure out where I'm going.

Proverbs 14:8 (New Living Translation)
The prudent understand where they are going but fools deceive themselves.

How did I get here? Why does this keep happening to me? Am I ever going to be successful?

First off, we have to understand what prudent means; it's not a word we use a lot in our current culture. Prudence means showing care for your future. You give forethought to your day, week, or year. Let me give a little context: a prudent person would be driving down the road and see a pothole.

They would then begin to start a thought process that would help them to be able to navigate safely around it, saving them the money, energy, and a scheduling conflict that could mess up the plans of the day.

The simpleton gets jarred by driving directly over the pothole at the speed limit, then the simpleton wonders why their tire is flat and the wheel is bent, and now their car needs an alignment.

All in all, they have to spend time, energy, and money, all because they did not think things through. If this is you, don't beat yourself up. I used to do this all the time. However, applying the principles found in Proverbs has helped me create a lifestyle of prudence as I pursue wisdom, knowledge, and discernment.

Truth: God created you in his image, and he created you to be a prudent person.

Declaration: I will begin to plan not only my day but my years as well, creating goals for each season of my life. God has given me a future.

Application: Take three heart desires and develop a plan to accomplish all of them. It could be a one-year plan or a multifaceted five-year plan. If this is beyond you at the moment to find a friend or mentor that has proven themselves as a "planner" and ask for guidance.

Notes:

_____

_____

_____

_____

_____

_____

_____

_____

_____

_____

_____

_____

_____

Chapter Fifteen

Do you understand the words that are coming out of my mouth?

Hey there, you are attractive!

Proverbs 15:2–4 (New Living Translation)

The tongue of the wise makes knowledge appealing, but the mouth of a fool belches out foolishness.

Can I really grow in knowledge? Does it really make me appealing? I look good!

Yes, and yes! Two things, when you listen to someone who is speaking the truth, I am talking Godly truth that you feel to your very core, even if it is not what you want to hear, you are like "Oh, I need to listen; this is good." When normally we shrug it off, the spirit of wisdom catches our attention, and as we begin to listen and take note of the info, our spiritual DNA gets rewritten in his glory.

Over the course of getting my doctorate, there were some professors that really just caught my spirit, and I just had to listen. Even in undergrad, I had an English professor that just got me excited for learning how to write better.

In contrast, how many of us have kids that let a big burp out right at the dinner table without really noticing. Then they let out a nervous giggle. That is how our mouths are when we partner with folly; we spew out words that we cannot take back, and they impact others negatively.

Speaking mean words hurts; we need to be diving into wisdom knowledge and discernment and think about what we are saying.

Truth: Ask, seek, knock, and wisdom will come to you! God is not a respecter of persons; what he will do for one, he will do for another.

Declaration: I am growing in wisdom, knowledge, and discernment as I study this devotional!

Application: Develop a habit of reading a Proverb a day and taking at least one verse from each day to apply to your daily life.

Notes:

_____

_____

_____

_____

_____

_____

_____

_____

_____

_____

_____

_____

_____

_____

_____

Chapter Sixteen

Fear does not always mean we are to be scared.

Run for your life, or better yet, run to your life.

Proverbs 16:6 (New Living Translation)

Unfailing love and faithfulness make atonement for sin. By fearing the Lord, people avoid evil.

Isn't God supposed to scare me? What can love really do? Am I still sinful?

Fear of the Lord is a complicated topic. The more I have learned about it, the more questions I have. Fear of the Lord is the foundation of wisdom. However, the word fear that is used here is a pregnant word. It means awe, wonder, splendor, majesty, and yes, fear. So let us paraphrase this verse with this enhanced definition. Unfailing love and faithfulness make atonement for sin. By staying close to the fear, staying in the wonderment of the Lord, being captivated by his awe and majesty, we will avoid evil.

You see, the "fear" of the Lord has nothing to do with its twisted counterpart like what you would see in a haunted house. Functioning in fear (proper definition) keeps us from doing evil or getting caught up in sin. When we are tempted, fear or "wisdom" is right there, saying "Run for your life; GET AWAY!" This is literally what I hear when sin or temptation comes knocking on my door.

When temptation comes I will start worshipping or reading my bible out loud if I cannot physically leave. I'm happy to run when temptation comes because of the love that Jesus has for me, which in turn empowers me to love him so much I steer clear of sin.

32   DR. JASON HIMMELBERGER

Truth: The fear of the Lord is not necessarily unpleasant!

Declaration: I am in awe of what God is doing in my life! Fear of the Lord helps me, love, to the point of holiness.

Application: Practice recognizing the awe wonder and majesty of God throughout your day. You don't have to stop what you are doing; however, pause and reflect on the moment and just praise him in his presence

Notes:

_____

_____

_____

_____

_____

_____

_____

_____

_____

_____

_____

_____

_____

_____

_____

Chapter Seventeen

A little water over the dam never hurts anyone, right???

What were we even mad about?

Proverbs 17:14 (New Living Translation)

Starting a quarrel is like opening a floodgate, so stop before a dispute breaks out.

If it's in the Bible, then yes, it's true; take a lesson from our science classes and even movies.

Think of any disaster-type movie with a dam. The dam bursts and the city below is in ruins. Staying with this scenario, your relationship is the city below the dam. Think of dams; they are pretty amazing to check out. I have been on several dam tours, lol, I'm reminded of my younger days with movies I probably should not have watched due to their crude humor, such as *National Lampoon's Vacation*. Dam jokes on the dam.

The reality is that we have to be really careful. Being married for twenty-nine years now, I am still learning when to say something and when to just let it go and be quiet. Starting an argument is like opening the dam, and everything just starts to flow out with a very strong force behind it. Don't even say one word because as soon as little water comes out, it will take too much pressure to try to close it back up.

Once you release one negative word, the argument is going to come, and an hour later, you will be wondering how it even started. That is this scripture in action. One thing, I have learned in relational communication is when I really want to say something, the most amazing tool is to bite my tongue.

DR. JASON HIMMELBERGER

Truth: I can communicate effectively with those around me, just as Jesus did.

Declaration: I am an effective communicator; I use wisdom to know when to speak and when not to.

Application: Practice with a friend or spouse; let them know what you are trying to do, and allow them into the process of knowing when and when not to speak.

Notes:

_____

_____

_____

_____

_____

_____

_____

_____

_____

_____

_____

_____

_____

_____

_____

Chapter Eighteen

How do my eyes look? Are they on point?

They are not even worth my time; very dangerous words.

Proverbs 18:12 (New Living Translation)
Haughtiness goes before destruction; humility precedes honor.

What is haughty? Does humility precede honor?

No, we are not talking about beautiful people; we are not even talking about physical appearances. Haughtiness means to think you are better than those around you. We are talking about pride and arrogance. Jesus came in the spirit of pride to lord over His people, right? Nope! He came as a vulnerable baby to serve His people.

With age, He became a man, continuing to serve and love. You see, humility goes before or rules over pride and arrogance. Humility makes a way for you in your life and circumstances. Humility will bring favor to your life. Humility will also allow you to grow in the Lord. God always makes a way when we take on his spirit. Remember this, pride tears down to lift itself; humility lifts others around up without fear of who's is better or superior. With God, we all get a promotion!

Truth: Humility makes a way for you on a daily basis.

Declaration: I will be more and more humble in seeing breakthroughs in my life.

Application: Start lifting those in your peer group; start encouraging them throughout the day and serve them.

Notes:

_____

_____

_____

_____

_____

_____

_____

_____

_____

_____

_____

_____

_____

_____

Chapter Nineteen

You were created to love!

Tractor beam locked on, wisdom is coming our way!

Proverbs 19:8 (New Living Translation)

To acquire wisdom is to love yourself; people who cherish understanding will prosper.

So in the kingdom of God, is there a thing such as a self-love? Isn't that self-serving?

Loving yourself is an aspect of God's Kingdom. God is love, and you were created in his image. Therefore, to love yourself is to love God. Remember, how you relate to God is how you will relate to others. Another aspect to remember is that the pursuit of wisdom is beneficial to yourself and those around you. Wisdom will give you the right words to say when helping a grieving friend.

Wisdom will help you decide if you are to take the new job or not. Understanding and wisdom go hand in hand; they are cousins. These two things will help you to prosper. As you prosper, those around will begin to prosper as a by-product of you being a life-giving fountain to those around you!

Truth: Wisdom is valuable to you and those around you!

Declaration: I cherish wisdom so that I can help those around me.

Application: Begin to journal about current conversations and real-life situations, asking God for help in those specific conversations. When finished, if they are life-giving, share them with the person, first explaining to them that you are practicing growing in wisdom and hearing the Lord for others.

Notes:

_____

_____

_____

_____

_____

_____

_____

_____

_____

_____

_____

_____

_____

_____

_____

_____

Chapter Twenty

Shining like diamonds

I'm a 14 carat.

Proverbs 20:15 (New Living Translation)
Wise words are more valuable than much gold and many rubies.

Really words are valuable? More than gold? What is heaven's value system?

The Bible uses many different illustrations to get us to understand the value of a word. Some are literal and some are figurative. In this case, it's both. Have you ever had a friend speak the right words in a specific situation? Words that were the tangible key to your breakthrough? Let me tell you, I would pay money to have that in every situation I face, wouldn't you?

Well, we can be the deliverer of the timely words for those around us by learning this value system of God's kingdom. Wisdom is much more valuable than all those worldly gems.

That is what I always ask for in prayer. You can't just pray for these things. You have to be desperate for them; if you ask for it, you have to follow the advice. Be willing to go through the process.

For example: If I get a job, I don't just get a paycheck, I have to show up and submit to the rules set by the management team, the schedule, the code of conduct, etc. Submission is a powerful thing; Jesus was submitted to the father.

Truth: God places a high value on words, and so should we.

Declaration: I seek wisdom to be a blessing and receive blessings.

Application: When a friend is going through "the stuff," be slow to speak and actually ask God for the words and strategies to speak, then listen and journal His responses to share with them.

Notes:

_____

_____

_____

_____

_____

_____

_____

_____

_____

_____

_____

_____

_____

_____

_____

_____

Chapter Twenty-One

Hey, I know a shortcut!

WOW, that's a lot of extra work; are you really going to do it that way?

Proverbs 21:5 (New Living Translation)

Good planning and hard work lead to prosperity, but hasty shortcuts lead to poverty.

Is it really worth it, to go the extra mile? What will it profit me? Working faster leads to poverty?

This is tangible in so many ways. Let's use a construction analogy. If I cut corners, trying to save a little time and money, then the inspector comes along and says, "Where's the permit?" Or the wall is not built to the code; you will have to tear it all apart and redo it to the standard that the inspector demands. In the end, the project will be behind schedule and will end up costing you more money than it would have to begin with.

Don't cut corners. It will cost you and may take all of your profit that you planned on making. This analogy translates to so many things that come at us in our lives. Often in our life opportunities come along that tempt us to do things the quick way. Reading Proverbs daily will help you to grow in wisdom and discern the pitfalls that may be tempting us.

Truth: God has equipped you to pay attention to the details!

Declaration: I have an eye for the small stuff that matters, and I profit in all my dealings.

Application: Rather than just doing a project from the hip, make a sketch, a build sheet, and a budget. See if you can pay attention to the details. This could be a backyard project or a shopping list. Invite the Holy Spirit into the process.

Notes:

_____

_____

_____

_____

_____

_____

_____

_____

_____

_____

_____

_____

_____

_____

Chapter Twenty-Two

Well done, you did a great job!

You have been working hard, and I've noticed., I'm giving you a promotion.

Proverbs 22:29 (New Living Translation)
Do you see any truly competent workers? They will serve kings rather than work for ordinary people.

Should I work really hard for my boss? Is it that big of a deal? I get my work done.

This is a great proverb to apply to our everyday lives. So many of us work for a paycheck but how many of us work to serve our boss and get a paycheck in the process. You see there is a difference. I've always tried to take great care of the company that I am working for. Jesus came as a servant, and I strive to do the same, regardless of the paycheck.

As you begin to go the extra mile for your employer over time, they will take note and you will be promoted. The term king in this verse can be literal or a higher-level manager or even a business owner. Taking care of the company can help you in becoming the owner's right-hand person.

Truth: God has created you to be spiritual royalty which will translate in the natural realm.

Declaration: I will work harder this year and see the reward from serving my employer.

Application: Go the extra mile, stay a bit longer, put in the extra effort in all that you do, whether it be serving at church or in the workplace, and yes, even at school.

Notes:

_____

_____

_____

_____

_____

_____

_____

_____

_____

_____

_____

_____

_____

_____

Chapter Twenty-Three

Celebrate good times. C'mon!

Experience joy over and over.

Proverbs 23:15–16 (New Living Translation)
My child, if your heart is wise, my own heart will rejoice!
Everything in me will celebrate when you speak what is right.

How do I make the Lord happy? What does God's happiness look like?

As a pastor, I am asked all the time: How can I make God happy? Well, the answer is hidden in plain sight. Do you see it? If we pursue wisdom and follow in the Lord and his principles. If we continually grow, not allowing ourselves to become a stagnant tide pool. By continuing to "grow" in our relationship, we will make the Lord happy. Fear of the Lord is the beginning of wisdom. God is so good in how He operates. He says, "pursue me, grow in me," and then He turns right back around us and showers us with His blessing and allows us to "use" wisdom in all we do.

DR. JASON HIMMELBERGER

Truth: I make God happy!

Declaration: I am growing in wisdom and causing the Lord to rejoice!

Application: In Proverbs, you see a consistent theme: seek wisdom. So, in this application, let's pray this prayer together. Father God, help me to grow in your wisdom that my heart may know you more. Help me to be more sensitive to your kingdom.

Notes:

_____

_____

_____

_____

_____

_____

_____

_____

_____

_____

_____

_____

_____

_____

_____

_____

Chapter Twenty-Four

There is gold in here!

Check, check, I hear you loud and clear.

Proverbs 24:3–4 (New Living Translation):

A house is built by wisdom and becomes strong through good sense.

Through knowledge, its rooms are filled with all sorts of precious riches and valuables.

Ok, so I get wisdom, and my house is strong, and I get valuable things for my life?

So, we know that wisdom, knowledge, and discernment are a type and cast of the Trinity Godhead—Father, Son, Holy Spirit. Your house will be built strong by the Godhead. This is a rather obvious statement; however, when we begin to break the statement down a bit, that is when the depth of the word comes.

Through Godly wisdom, our house will become strong, strong in every way. If our life is the house then as God blesses the rooms everything will get better, yes maybe over time. Our life will get better relationally, financially, emotionally; even health will be established in your life. You will have strength in every sense of the word. Maybe not all at once; however, in direct reaction to your pursuit of his word and will for your life.

Truth: God wants to fill your house with his treasure.

Declaration: God wants to fill my house with his accessible treasure, so I can have a strong house.

Application: Be a decided person, who is pursuing the wisdom of God that is made available to us all.

Notes:

_____

_____

_____

_____

_____

_____

_____

_____

_____

_____

_____

_____

_____

_____

Chapter Twenty-Five

Want to play a game?

It's time to play the ultimate game of hide and seek; only royalty gets to play. Yes, you are royalty

Proverbs 25:2 (New Living Translation)

It is God's privilege to conceal things and the king's privilege to discover them.

Why does God conceal things? How do I find the hidden things?

This is one of my favorites. God loves to hide things in plain sight for us to find. Once you see them, you will ask yourself, "How did I not see that before?" Wisdom, Knowledge, and Discernment will help you to find the hidden things that are available to all Christ-followers. God loves to conceal these little mysteries so that we can exercise learning responsibility, so we might grow in understanding.

We have a responsibility to not only receive Christ but also to publicly acknowledge Him; in addition, to also internally acknowledge Him spiritually and personally. We are kings and queens—spiritually speaking—and it is our job to gain understanding so that we might teach others.

Truth: God hides things in plain sight. He has equipped you to find them.

Declaration: I am a treasure hunter in God's kingdom, finding the precious jewels of heaven hidden in plain sight.

Application: Ask, seek, knock, pound on the door of the hidden things of God to get revelation, healing, and increase.

Notes:

_____

_____

_____

_____

_____

_____

_____

_____

_____

_____

_____

_____

_____

_____

_____

Chapter Twenty-Six

Incoming!!! Watch out! Wow, that was close!

Man that thing almost got me

Proverbs 26:2 (New Living Translation)

Like a fluttering sparrow or a darting swallow, an undeserved curse will not land on its intended victim.

Are curses real? Undeserved curse? How do I get protected?

The reality is, we are at war! With an unseen enemy that is out to steal, kill, and destroy anything and everything that is made available to us. This unseen enemy is more visible than you would think.

Reading Proverbs every day will help you grow in wisdom, knowledge, and discernment. This discernment will increase your ability to "see" this unseen reality. And with the authority that is given and placed right inside you. You can cause that bullet of the enemy to curve just enough to miss you.

Truth: Holiness causes the bullets of the enemy to go off track.

Declaration: I can see the shots of the enemy from a mile away and command them to fall before they get to their intended target!

Application: In your devotional time, ask God to reveal the shots from the enemy that you haven't seen. Ask Him to heal them, so you can move on free and strong into the plans he has for you.

Notes:

_____

_____

_____

_____

_____

_____

_____

_____

_____

_____

_____

_____

_____

_____

_____

Chapter Twenty-Seven

Help, I've fallen and I can't get up!

Hello, my name is Jason, I'm a grateful believer and I struggle with sin.

Proverbs 27:8 (New Living Translation / The Passion Translation)
A person who strays from home is like a bird that strays from its nest.

What happens when we fall? Can we find our way back? Does God just open up his arms to us again?

I added the passion translation to this particular verse because the word translated from "stray" to "fall" seems to fit much better contextually. Let's face facts, we have all fallen throughout this journey we call life. The beautiful reality of this relationship with the Godhead is the truth that He is there with open arms as we turn away from the thing that we allowed to trip us up, even though it grieves him. God, the Father, sent His son to wipe us clean of all our unrighteousness.

The bible also says in Prover 24:16 though the Godly may fall they get up seven times. So yes God does really just open up his arms to us again.

Truth: God forgives you of that thing you did. You know the one I am talking about, the one you don't want anyone to know about. He loves you and cares for your well-being.

Declaration: The blood of Jesus shed on the cross was more than enough to cover my fall.

Application: Begin to take stock of the freedom that is available to us through Jesus. Take a daily inventory, actually repenting of the stuff that needs to go allowing a beautiful thing to take place.

Notes:

_____

_____

_____

_____

_____

_____

_____

_____

_____

_____

_____

_____

_____

_____

Chapter Twenty-Eight

Ahhhh! I'm scared! I can't do that.

I was so scared, but I did it! Wow, that was crazy!

Proverbs 28:01 (New Living Translation)

The wicked run away when no one is chasing them, but the godly are as bold as lions.

Why do we get so scared to do something? What are we really afraid of?

The wicked run. To be wicked is to operate outside of God's parameters that he has for us. Just imagine for a moment that heaven was one acre, and in that acre, we had access to all that heaven had. Boldness, healing, breakthrough, provision were all within this one acre.

Going outside of this perimeter meant you did not have access to the "thing." You could only use them while you were there. Staying in the presence of God allows us to function outside of the world standards. We don't have to run; we can stand boldly with God's help.

Truth: You don't have to run any longer; stay strong, and be bold in the Lord!

Declaration: I will stand and be courageous! Through Christ, I can do more than I think!

Application: Pray daily for more boldness. By doing this consistently, you will begin to see a breakthrough. You will look back and say to yourself, "Oh my, I used to do this?"

Notes:

_____

_____

_____

_____

_____

_____

_____

_____

_____

_____

_____

_____

_____

_____

_____

_____

Chapter Twenty-Nine

But what will people think?

That's not going to go over well, or is it?

Proverbs 29:25 (New Living Translation)

Fearing people is a dangerous trap, but trusting the Lord means safety.

Is this a real thing? Have you already fallen in? How do I get out?

This is something that I will admit. It takes work to walk without the fear of man. The fear of man is such an easy trap to fall into, especially in ministry and business. This is a problem for everyone. Our kids while they're at school are constantly subjected to the idea of being concerned about what others think about them. Even while writing this book, I have the thoughts such as, are people going to like it?

Are they going to be blessed by it? What will they think of me? The reality is that none of that matters, only what Papa God says about me. Was I faithful with what he gave me to do? Father God has set the standard for how we are to live. His thoughts are the only ones that we should be concerned with.

The question put forth to us is, do I do everything the Lord is calling me to accomplish even if people are going to judge me?

The fear of man will put you in a corner, and you will be placed in a time-out, missing out on what the Lord has for us. We as believers need to be aware of the dogs of doom standing at the doors of destiny, trying to scare us away from the door.

Truth: God will keep you safe.

Declaration: Jesus is cheering me on. He wants to see me succeed in all my endeavors.

Application: What's the one thing that you have been wanting to do; however, you have been afraid to do it? Pray and ask the Lord if you are ready to do it, assuming you are, make an action plan to start the process; just take baby steps.

Notes:

_____

_____

_____

_____

_____

_____

_____

_____

_____

_____

_____

_____

_____

_____

Chapter Thirty

I Tarzan, U Jane.

"Are you tired? Do you lack knowledge?"

Proverbs 30:1–3 (New Living Translation)

The sayings of Agur son of Jakeh contain this message. I am weary, O God; I am weary and worn out, O God. I am too stupid to be human, and I lack common sense. I have not mastered human wisdom, nor do I know the Holy One.

Can you relate to this passage? Have you ever felt like less than yourself? What does lacking knowledge mean?

I believe that all of us can relate to not feeling like ourselves due to life circumstances. Recently I was doing some ministry in Zambia. Just before this trip, I also went to Charleston, South Carolina to attend a conference and visit a good friend, so this international's trip was already long before it even got going.

Then eighteen hours before I was to return, the Netherlands invoked a travel ban, due to their COVID-19 cases, which meant my flight was suddenly canceled. Traveling from nation to nation for days and days can make you feel like a beast more than a man; however, God, as He always does, takes care of us.

I was introduced to a pastor who was a farmer, and he invited me to stay with him for a couple of days while the dust settled and I could arrange travel home. Rest is such an important thing to make sure that we keep a priority in our lives! This "rest" allows us to clear our mind of the junk and just focus on God, that is when the revelation comes!

DR. JASON HIMMELBERGER

Truth: God provides access to supernatural rest amidst the chaos of our lives for us to grow in the wisdom of the reality of the oneness that we have in Him.

Declaration: I will continue to grow in the knowledge of the things of God.

Application: Amid chaotic situations, ask the Lord for rest and insight on what he has for you.

Notes:

_____

_____

_____

_____

_____

_____

_____

_____

_____

_____

_____

_____

_____

_____

_____

_____

Chapter Thirty-One

So wait, I can be a Proverbs-31 man?

Proverbs 31:16–17 (New Living Translation)

She goes to inspect a field and buys it; with her earnings, she plants a vineyard. She is energetic and strong, a hard worker.

So wait, this applies to me as a man? You mean women have authority? Yes and yes!

First off, let me address the gender issue. Being contextually accurate, we have to understand that the word of God is for all people. Galatians says that there is neither male nor female in Christ Jesus. Traditionally, this passage has been used to keep woman in subjection to man.

To interpret this passage in this way, pretending it only applies to females, robs a man of massive blessing. So again, this all applies to both genders. Just paraphrase what is written to be appropriate for your gender.

Your spouse trusts you. A Proverbs-31 spouse has authority in the relationship. Something that is supposed to happen when we get married is we are to honor each other. We honor the person by trusting them to make kingdom-minded decisions that will befit our family honorably.

Could you imagine having a little side hustle and saving enough money to buy property and start another business on the property without asking your spouse?

A Proverbs-31 person is a business mogul. By selling their wares in the market, they have a lot to manage. Are you energetic and strong and a hard worker? A Proverbs-31 person is! This proverb gives you a glimpse of what the Lord wants for you. It's really important we build equality in our relationship to one another by inviting each other into the decisions that are to be made.

Truth: God is calling you to be a Proverbs-31 person!

Declaration: I have supernatural energy and strategy to have multiple streams of income for my family.

Application: Talk with your spouse about how you can empower each other, keeping in mind that Proverbs-31 is for both of you. If you are not married yet, start applying these principles now to set yourself up for success for the future.

Notes:

_____

_____

_____

_____

_____

_____

_____

_____

_____

_____

_____

_____

_____

_____